CONTENTS

Words that appear in **bold italic** in the text are explained in
the glossary on page 30.

WHO WERE THE AZTECS?

The first people to enter the Americas came from Asia around 30,000 years ago. People were 'hunters and gatherers' in those days, meaning they lived by hunting wild animals and gathering roots and berries. They were often on the move, following herds of animals and looking for new sources of plants.

By the time they had reached Central America many tribes had become farmers – they grew their own crops. This meant people did not have to keep moving and could stay in one place.

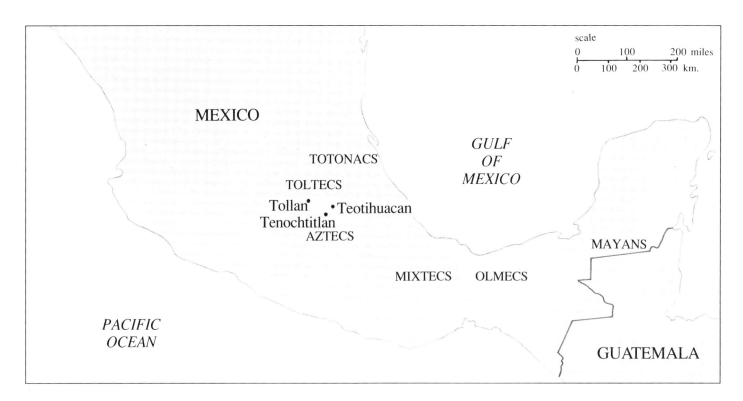

Many groups of people moved into Mexico, which in **ancient** times was known as 'Anahuac' meaning 'the land between the waters'. By 1200 one of these groups had developed into a separate tribe called the Tenochas, which we know as the Aztecs.

However, at this time all the best land had been taken by other, stronger tribes and this meant the Aztecs had a long period of wandering and searching for a suitable place to settle. All the other tribes of Mexico at the time viewed the Aztecs with great suspicion. The Aztecs were often attacked and pushed out of land they tried to claim for themselves.

Finally, the Aztecs settled on a number of small islands in the middle of Lake Texcoco, where by 1325 they started building a fine city called Tenochtitlan. The surrounding countryside was linked to the city by a number of **causeways** across the lake.

As you will see, Tenochtitlan was full of magnificent buildings, such as palaces and temples. This temple has survived in another part of Mexico, but the main temple of Tenochtitlan probably looked very similar. Study it carefully. How was it built? Such a temple would have required great **engineering** skills.

From this base of Tenochtitlan – meaning 'place of the Tenochas' – a great **empire** was built that would last 200 years. It was an empire of great invention and beauty, but also of customs and beliefs which we might think cruel.

The story of the ► Aztec empire is an exciting one. As we trace its history we will see a lot of objects from the time – what **archaeologists** call **artefacts**. Artefacts help us to find out how the Aztecs lived.

One reason that we know so much about the Aztecs is because they drew wonderful books called Codices. The Aztecs did not write with words, but used pictures instead. This is a page from the Codex Cospi, showing the Gods of the Sun and Darkness. Can you work out which god is which? The beautiful colours in these pictures come from dyes made from vegetables and flowers.

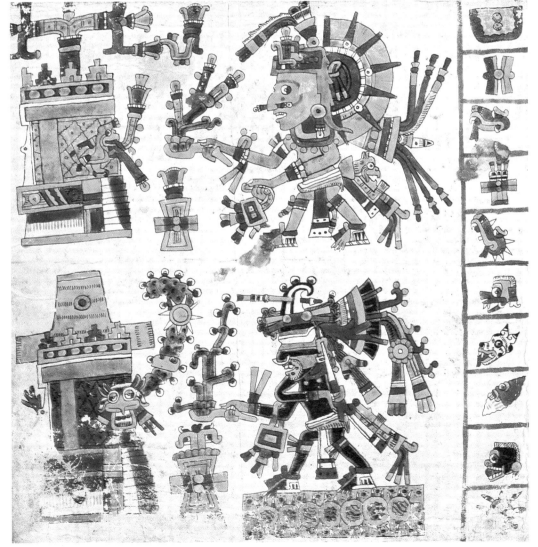

WORK AND FAMILY

Central to Aztec life was agriculture. We know that Tenochtitlan was built on small islands in a lake, so space for farming was limited. To overcome this problem the Aztecs built what have been called the floating gardens, or chinampas. These were woven reed baskets roughly 2.5 metres square filled with earth and fastened in shallow water. There were thousands of chinampas around the city and they provided vital areas of land for producing food. Mud was brought up from the bottom of the lake and used as *fertilizer*.

Goods that every family needed, such as grass mats, pottery and canoes, would be **bartered** in a market. Throughout history all farming *civilizations* have used vast amounts of pottery. Do you know what it was used for? Think of all the crockery you use at home. Pottery was used for storage, cooking and eating. Pots like these were often decorated by women in the home.

◄ Can you see what crop is being grown here? It is maize – what we call corn on the cob. Maize was made into the main Aztec food: tortillas. These were flat, baked corn cakes, eaten by all families every day. The picture shows the planting, **hoeing** and harvesting in the maize field, which was called the milpa. Aztec farmers helped each other in the fields. The land was not owned by one person but by groups of families called clans. As we shall see, war was very important to the Aztecs and if a farmer was away fighting, his fields were looked after by others of his clan.

This statue seems ► to show a worker in the fields. He is carrying maize cobs and the heavy basket is fixed around his head. As proof of the importance of maize, this is a statue of a very important god – Quetzalcoatl, whom you will learn more of later. As 'God of Life', Quetzalcoatl helped crops grow, which explains the five maize cobs on his back.

7

◀ The family was a very important unit in Aztec life, but it had clear duties to the clan. Aztec men married at about the age of 20, women at 16. This picture is of a newly-married couple. They have tied their cloaks together as a sign of their marriage. 'Tied together' was an expression in Aztec society for marriage. When married they could live in either the man's clan or the woman's. Women did have certain rights in Aztec society – far ahead of many women elsewhere in the world at the same time! A woman could own property, obtain a divorce if she was badly treated and go to a court to plead justice. Once divorced she could marry again, although if widowed she had to re-marry inside her clan.

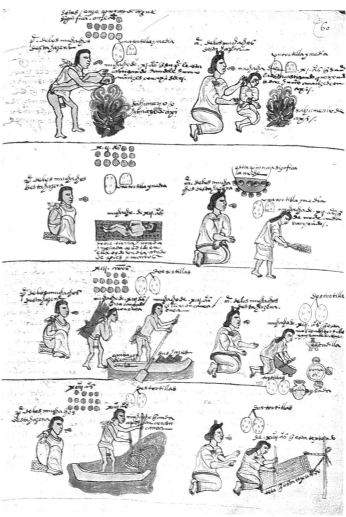

This picture shows the punishments given to ▶ naughty children! Also it tells us what skills older children learned. What is happening to the boy and girl at the top? The blue dots tell us their age. For their wrongdoing they are being held over a smoking fire – a very unusual punishment by our standards! The next pair shows a boy being forced to lie out on damp grass and a girl having to sweep up. In the bottom four pictures you can see more children being trained in other skills. Can you work out how old they are and what they are being taught?

THE GREAT CITY

Look at the ▶ splendid title page from the Codex Cospi. It shows how the city of Tenochtitlan was founded. The bird perched on the cactus branch in the centre is an eagle. This comes from a very old and important Aztec legend. One of the gods told the tribe to search for a swamp where they would find an eagle on a cactus with a snake in its claw. This was to be the site where the Aztecs were to build their city – Tenochtitlan.

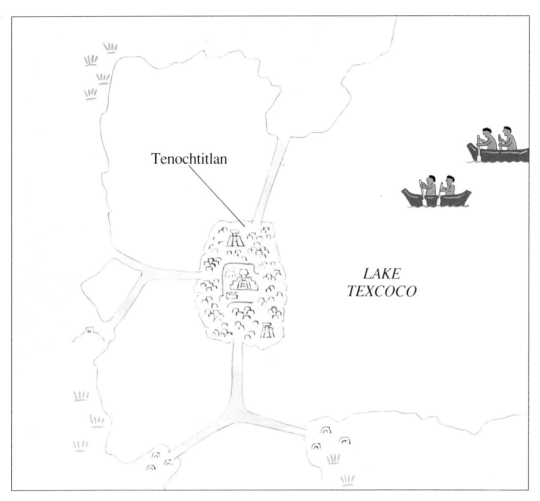

Tenochtitlan

LAKE TEXCOCO

◀ A visitor to Tenochtitlan would immediately notice the causeways (there were four of them) serving the city. They were cleverly built, and had a system of drawbridges which could be lifted in the case of attack. At least two carried an **aqueduct** that supplied the city with fresh water. As soon as the water reached the city square, it was piped off to other areas or collected by people with jugs and carriers.

Many people ▶ lived in the city – what would their homes have been like? Sadly, none exist today, but archaeologists have discovered what they may have looked like. Poorer people's houses were probably simple wattle-and-daub buildings with a thatched roof. The wattle walls were made of intertwined branches and daub is the smearing of mud and animal dung over the branches.

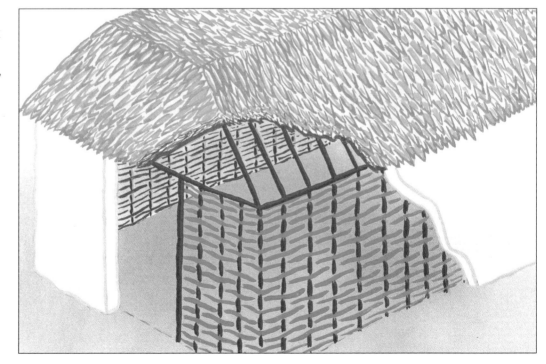

The central point of the city was the great temple of Huitzilopochtli, the Sun God. It no longer exists, but this is a temple that has been rebuilt to show what an Aztec temple looked like. What is it made of? Does it remind you of any other ancient building? Placed at the top of this stepped structure was the God-House, containing statues and images of the gods.

Gods

Aztec gods demanded human *sacrifices*. The only way to provide a constant supply of sacrificial victims was by war! To the Aztecs, the gods demanded permanent war. The most important god was Huitzilopochtli. Aztec priests taught the people that Huitzilopochtli was a powerful warrior who fought with the moon and the stars to win each new day. If he was not fed with human blood and hearts, he would be defeated and the world would end.

▲ Look at this beautiful but fearsome knife. The blade is razor-sharp flint and the handle is *turquoise mosaic*. With this type of knife the priests cut open the victim's chest while he was held spread-eagled on the sacrificial stone, and removed his heart. This happened at the very top of the temple, next to the God-House.

What took place next can be seen here. ▶
After the victim's heart was cut out, the priest cut off the victim's head. The snakes falling from the head represent the blood being spilt. The heads were then stored in the temple.

The priests who carried out these sacrifices were strange-looking men. Their bodies were painted black all over and they had long hair which was never washed or cut.

Huitzilopochtli had a **deputy** called Ixtilton. This rather sinister mask, made of obsidian – a dark, glassy rock from volcanoes – is believed to be of him. The colour of the mask is just right for Ixtilton's job. His name means 'Little Black One' and it was believed that he visited children in bed at night and covered them in darkness, which made them sleep soundly. **13**

Another important ▶
god was Quetzalcoatl.
In this carving he is
wearing his cone-
shaped hat, a
necklace, earrings and
a jewel in the shape
of a star on his chest.
This jewel stands for
the wind, because
Quetzalcoatl was the
God of the Wind. Do
you notice any
unusual decoration?
An object, probably a
piece of jewellery,
has pierced his nose.

Time was very ► important to the Aztecs. One of their calendars contained eighteen months of twenty days. This picture is an engraving of a great calendar stone, made 200 years after the Aztec Empire to show how the Aztecs measured time. It has the twenty day-names on it, and the sun at the centre. The real calendar stone would have been carved, and over 3 metres wide.

Time passed in a 52-year cycle. The years were counted by the placing of a stick or a rod in a bundle, one for each year. When fifty-two had been collected a new cycle began.

◄ An important ceremony called the tying up of the years was held at the end of each cycle.

Can you see the rods tied up in this carving? The real bundle of rods, tied up with a rope, was placed on to a fire and burnt. The *symbol* of the final year covered the rods, as you can see in the middle of the carving.

15

GAMES AND MUSIC

Aztec people loved to watch and play games. One of the most popular was 'Hachtli'. It was a very fierce and rough game. Hachtli was a cross between netball or basketball (but you could not use your hands) and rugby (because players were allowed to crash into each other!). The game was played in an I-shaped court, with walls about 2.5 metres high, and the aim was to get a rubber ball through a ring. This could only be done using elbows, legs and hips. The players may have worn some kind of padding on these parts of the body.

◄ This is one of the stone rings used as a goal in Hachtli. How is it different from a netball or basketball ring? The ring was placed vertically on the wall instead of horizontally and the team that managed to get the ball through the ring was the winner.

16

Music was important to the Aztecs. Do you know what these instruments are?

The beautifully carved instrument (above) is a drum. It was beaten on the two flaps at the top. You may have noticed that one flap is longer than the other. These gave different sounds when they were hit. The carved case shows a battle scene. Experts who have studied Aztec music believe it was very *rhythmic* and closely connected with dance.

The other two instruments (below) are flageolets, or small flutes. With the large number of ceremonies and festivals in Aztec life, music would have been very important.

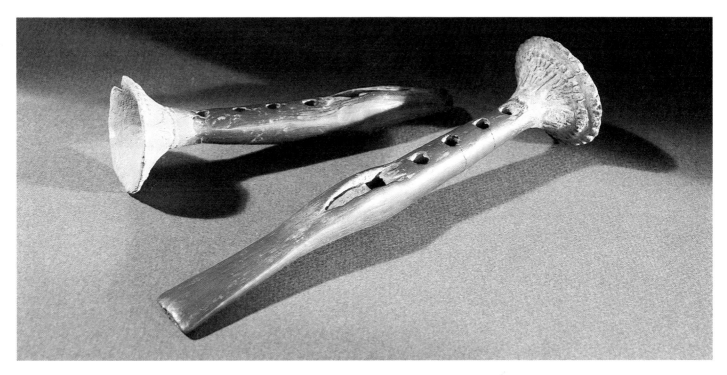

KNIGHTS AND WARRIORS

War was very important to the Aztecs. The gods demanded sacrifices, so prisoners of war had to be taken. When the Aztecs fought a battle they tried to frighten their enemy with drums and trumpets. They bombarded them with arrows and spears. The warriors then closed in and attacked with clubs. This usually made the enemy flee. If the leader was captured the battle ended immediately. The Aztecs soon built up a huge empire because of these successful wars.

What is this man wearing? Does it make him look fierce? In fact, he was a very important warrior, one of the Eagle Knights. The best Aztec warriors were divided into two groups, the Eagle and Jaguar Knights.

◄ Can you find a Jaguar Knight in this group? One of the jobs he had to carry out was to go out and look for the enemy and report back with information about him. Try and find the Eagle Knight in this group as well. To become a warrior was a great honour in Aztec society. At fifteen young boys were taught how to fight and use all the different weapons. Each young **recruit** followed an experienced warrior into battle to learn the art of warfare.

What weapons did Aztecs use? Although ► these weapons look like thick swords, they are in fact wooden clubs, made deadly by sharp obsidian flakes wedged in their sides. To defend themselves in battle the warriors have round wooden shields covered with animal skin.

This photograph shows you a decorated shield. It is a back shield from the Toltecs, one of the tribes who lived in Mexico before the Aztecs. Aztec shields were very similar. Warriors wore them to protect their backs when they were fighting hand-to-hand.

Aztec warriors also ▶ carried one or two wooden throwing spears. Like the clubs, these spears, held by the warriors at the top and bottom of this picture, have been made more dangerous with sharp obsidian blades on the sides.

Spears were much more deadly when launched from spear throwers called atlatls. Look at the groove in the back of the atlatl on the right. The spear was slotted into this and then held by the two-fingered grip. In battle, when the atlatl was hurled, it made the arm of the thrower seem longer. This meant that the spears were thrown at a great speed and also improved the aim of the warrior. Other weapons used by warriors included bows and arrows.

▼ A sign of the Aztec victory was the burning of the enemy temple. Look at this detail from the Codex Cospi. Can you pick out the defeated warriors and the destruction of the temples in the background? Any prisoners who were not sacrificed were usually sold to be slaves.

colhuacan. pueblo.   tenayucan. pueblo/

APPEARANCE

We have learnt a lot concerning the Aztec way of life, but what did they look like? Not surprisingly, most people took a great deal of trouble over their appearance.

Young, single women wore their hair long and straight. This mask shows a fashion popular with married women. Look carefully at the mask's forehead. Can you see the plaited hair curling around to the back of the head where it stands up? Colourful ribbons were also woven into the hair.

Most women ▶ wore wrap-around skirts, fastened by a belt. These skirts were fringed with ornaments to cover the knees. On top of the skirt a woman wore a colourful **poncho**, fringed with tassels and split at the centre for her head. Although this is a statue of Lady Precious Green, a very important **fertility** goddess, it does show some of these fashions. Notice her headdress and earrings and the tassels attached to her poncho.

▲ All the men wore **loin-cloths**, often with an **embroidered** flap at the front and back. Over this they wore a cloak or cape, often decorated, which was held in position by a knot over the shoulder. Everyone wore sandals and the straps were usually made of jaguar skin.

When attending ▶ special ceremonies, women would decorate their faces. Look at these small objects. Can you work out the designs, especially on the two on the right? They are pottery stamps and were painted with bright colours and then pressed on the face. This must have looked very striking when different colours were used.

▲ Both men and women wore spectacular nose pendants. The centre of the nose was pierced so the pendant could be worn. These were more popular with men, but some women also wore them. This nose pendant is solid gold, with the face of a bearded god wearing a very fine headdress. The detail is very impressive, showing craftsmanship of the highest quality.

Great care was taken over turquoise and shell
work. These materials were used to decorate
masks, helmets and shields. The base to this
helmet is wood, which has been carefully inlaid
with shell and turquoise. Because this helmet
is so delicate it would probably have been used
only on special occasions, rather than for
protection.

MONTEZUMA AND THE GOD FROM THE EAST

At the top of Aztec society was the king. When he died his successor was chosen by the priests and army commanders. If you were part of the royal family, wise in the ways of religion and good in battle, you could be chosen. The king had a huge palace and army of people working for him. In 1502 a new king was chosen. He was Montezuma II and his name meant Courageous Lord.

This is the beautifully feathered headdress of Montezuma. He would have worn it when leading warriors into a battle.

Text within the illustration:
trono y estrado de moteccuma londe se sentava sor cortes ya sggon

(69)

moteccuma

casa londi orjo sentavan alos y. setenancia y chicimantla y colhuacom y eron sus amy gos y confede rados/ de moteccuma

casa londe aposenta son alos grandes senores de tezcuco toenbor y eron sus amygos de moteccuma

patio. delas casas feales de moteccuma

patio delas casas feales de moteccuma

sala del consejo se guerra

estas fojas tom subien do / tom a dar al patio delas casas de moteccuma y son estas figuras

estos quatro son como los dres del consejo de moteccuma / son bres salvios /

sala del consejo de moteccuma

plosteomtes / en grado se aple delos alts ante los consejo de moteccuma / se presenta los dres de moteccuma / parecse el consejo

Montezuma was a ► worried leader. There was a legend that the god Quetzalcoatl would return to earth. On the very day in the very year that his return had been predicted, the Spaniard Hernando Cortés with his **conquistadors** landed on the coast of Mexico, east of Tenochtitlan. The Aztecs believed that Cortés was in fact Quetzalcoatl, and welcomed him as the returning god. Montezuma lavished gifts on him, including this beautiful turquoise serpent.

This is a drawing ► by a Spanish artist of the welcome of Cortés in Tenochtitlan. Can you work out which one is meant to be Cortés? The woman on the right was very important. She is Dona Marina, a non-Aztec Mexican who came from the area where the Spaniards landed. She learnt Spanish quickly and became Cortés' translator, making conversations between Cortés and Montezuma possible.

▲ Montezuma's palace was in the heart of Tenochtitlan. It contained many rooms and if you study it carefully you will find Montezuma. In the room next to Montezuma's, stayed his personal bodyguard of 200 **chieftains.**

28

Tenochtitlan.

Cortés, who could not believe his good fortune, cleverly managed to rule the Aztecs through Montezuma. The Aztecs thought that Montezuma was betraying them, and he was killed. Cortés then attacked the city, and in August 1521 claimed Mexico for Spain. After 200 years the mighty Aztec empire lay in ruins.

GLOSSARY

Ancient   Belonging to a time long ago.

Aqueduct   A bridge for carrying water.

Archaeologists   People who study objects and remains from ancient times.

Artefacts   Objects, such as tools or pots, that archaeologists study to find out how people used to live.

Bartered   Exchanged goods for other goods rather than buying them with money.

Causeways   Raised roads or pathways across water.

Chieftains   Leaders of tribes or clans.

Civilizations   Particular groups of people and how they live.

Conquistadors   Spanish conquerors who claimed areas of South America for Spain 400 years ago.

Deputy   Someone who stands in for a leader.

Embroidered   Decorated with attractive stitching.

Empire   A group of smaller, weaker states ruled by a more powerful state.

Engineering   The design and construction of buildings, machines, roads and bridges.

Fertility   The ability for people to have children and for land to produce crops.

Fertilizer   Anything that helps make plants grow in soil.

Hoeing   Clearing weeds from between crops with a long-handled tool with a blade at the end.

Loin-cloths   Pieces of cloth worn around the hips.

Mosaic   A design made up of small pieces of stone or coloured glass.

Poncho   A square cloak made of cloth with a central hole for the head.

Recruit   Someone who is a new member of an army or organization.

Rhythmic   Music with a strong beat.

Sacrifices   Killing people (or sometimes animals) to offer to a god or goddess.

Symbol   Something that represents or stands for something else.

Turquoise   A greenish-blue stone, used in jewellery and decoration.

IMPORTANT DATES

c. 30,000 BC First groups of migrants reach the Americas

c. 800 BC Olmec civilization established in Mexico

c. 100 AD Toltec civilization established

510 Toltecs build Sun and Moon temples at Teotihuacan

1168 Aztec tribes migrate into the Anahuac valley

1250 Aztecs living close to Lake Texcoco

c. 1320 Aztecs occupy two islands in the middle of Lake Texcoco. Tenochtitlan – 'place of the Tenocha' – is founded

1481 Construction of huge temple to Huitzilopochtli, the Sun God, begins

1503 Montezuma II elected king

1519 Hernando Cortés arrives at Tenochtitlan

1521 Tenochtitlan captured and destroyed by Cortés and his conquistadors

1525 AZTEC EMPIRE IN RUINS

PRONUNCIATION

Here are some of the Aztec words you may find difficult to pronounce:

HUITZILOPOCHTLI – *Weet-sil-o-pocht-lee*
MONTEZUMA – *Mont-eh-soo-mah*
TENOCHTITLAN – *Ten-otch-teet-lan*
QUETZALCOATL – *Ket-sal-koat-l*
TEOTIHUACAN – *Tay-o-tee-wa-kan*
TEZCATLIPOCA – *Tess-kat-lee-pocka*
TEXCOCO – *Tess-koko*
TORTILLA – *Tort-ee-ya*

BOOKS TO READ

An Aztec Warrior by Anne Steel (Wayland, 1987) A book for children which describes the lifestyle of an Aztec warrior.

The Aztecs by Jacqueline Dineen (Heinemann Children's Reference, 1992) This book encourages children to use evidence to find out about the Aztec way of life.

The Aztecs by Robert Nicholson and Claire Watts (Two-Can Publishing, 1991) This book tells children about the daily life of the Aztecs.

Find out about Aztecs by Jill Hughes (Evans Brothers, 1992) An introduction to the Aztec civilization for children.

INDEX